976.2
FOR

Foran, Jill
Idaho

34880000 823448

IDAHO

Jill Foran

Published by Weigl Publishers Inc.
123 South Broad Street, Box 227
Mankato, MN   56002
USA
Web site: http://www.weigl.com

Library of Congress Cataloging-in-Publication Data

Foran, Jill.
    Idaho / Jill Foran.
        p. cm. -- (A kid's guide to American states)
    Includes index.
    ISBN 1-930954-33-6 (lib. bdg.)
    1. Idaho--Juvenile literature. [1. Idaho.] I. Title. II. Series.

F746.3 .F67 2001

2001017998

ISBN 1-930954-76-X (pbk.)

Printed in the United States of America
1 2 3 4 5 6 7 8 9 10   05 04 03 02 01

Project Coordinator
Michael Lowry
Substantive Editor
Jennifer Nault
Copy Editor
Bryan Pezzi
Designers
Warren Clark
Terry Paulhus
Layout
Carla Pelky
Photo Researcher
Diana Marshall

Photograph Credits
Every reasonable effort has been made to trace ownership and to obtain
permission to reprint copyright material. The publishers would be
pleased to have any errors or omissions brought to their attention so
that they may be corrected in subsequent printings.

Cover: Baldy Ski Mountain and cabin in Sun Valley (Marilyn "Angel" Wynn),
agate gemstone (Hemera Studios); **Scott Bauer/USDA:** pages 3B, 13T; **Boise
State University News Services:** page 15T; **City of Arco:** page 15BL; **Corbis
Corporation:** page 14BR; **Corel Corporation:** pages 3M, 7T, 7BL, 10T, 10B,
11T, 11BR, 24B, 28T, 28B, 29TR; **Digital Stock Corporation:** page 29TL;
EyeWire, Inc.: page 24B; **Idaho Department of Commerce:** pages 4T, 5T, 9T,
12T, 14BL, 20BL, 21B, 23B, 24T, 25T, 26B; **Idaho Potato Commission:** pages
7BR, 13B, 15BR; **Idaho State Historical Society Library and Archives:** pages
16BL, 16BR, 17T, 17BL, 18T, 18BR, 19T, 19BL, 19BR; **PhotoDisk, Inc.:** page
25BR; **Photofest:** pages 25BL, 27BL; **State of Idaho Secretary of State's Office:**
page 5BL; **Marilyn "Angel" Wynn:** pages 3T, 4BR, 4BL, 6T, 6B, 8T, 8BL, 8BR,
9B, 11BL, 12BL, 12BR, 14T, 16T, 17BR, 20T, 21T, 22T, 22BL, 22BR, 23T, 26T,
27T, 27BR.

CONTENTS

INTRODUCTION

In Idaho, water covers an area of about 823 square miles. Most of the water comes from the high mountain regions.

Idaho is in the northwestern part of the United States. It is a mountainous state, featuring magnificent forests, countless rivers and streams, and range after range of breathtaking peaks. Areas of open wilderness, such as meadows filled with wildflowers, add variety to the landscape.

Idaho is nicknamed "The Gem State." More than seventy-two types of **precious** and semi-precious stones are found in the state's mountains, valleys, and plains. These gemstones, along with valuable metals, such as silver, gold, and lead, are mined in Idaho. Gemstones are not the only things that shine in Idaho. Sparkling lakes, gleaming waterfalls, stunning landscapes, booming industries, and lively people help to make Idaho a true gem of a state.

QUICK FACTS

The capital of Idaho is Boise. It is in the southwestern part of the state.

The state song is "Here We Have Idaho."

One of the largest diamonds ever found in the United States was discovered in Idaho. The 20-carat diamond was discovered near McCall.

The mountain waters of Redfish Lake are so clear that the bottom can be seen at depths of over 20 feet.

Idaho has more than 59,890 miles of roads and highways.

Getting There

Idaho shares its borders with seven neighbors. Montana and Wyoming form Idaho's eastern boundaries, while Oregon and Washington form its western boundaries. Utah and Nevada lie to the south of Idaho, and Canada lies to the north.

A number of interstate highways run through Idaho. Interstate 15 and US 91, US 93 and US 95 connect the state from north to south, while Interstates 84, 86, and 90, and US 12, US 20, US 26, and US 30 travel east-west. All major cities in the state have commercial airports. The busiest airport in Idaho is the Boise Air Terminal. Two **transcontinental** railroads serve the state from east to west. Ships from the Pacific Ocean reach Idaho by traveling up the Snake and Columbia Rivers.

QUICK FACTS

Idaho is the fourteenth-largest state, covering an area of 83,574 square miles.

Idaho ranks as the forty-second state in population.

The square dance is Idaho's official state dance.

Idaho is the only state whose state seal was designed by a woman—Emma Sarah Etine Edwards. The seal's Latin motto, *Esto Perpetua*, means "It Is Forever."

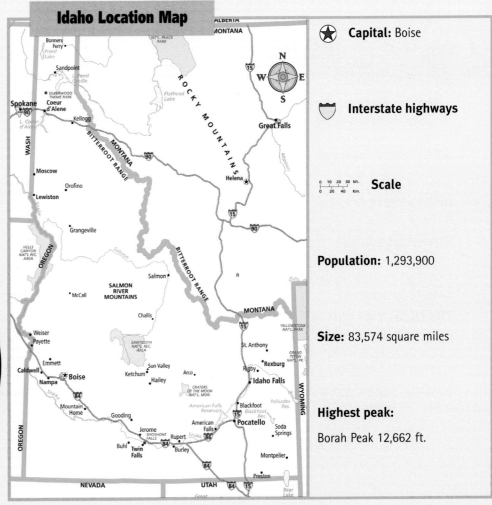

Idaho Location Map

Capital: Boise

Interstate highways

Scale

Population: 1,293,900

Size: 83,574 square miles

Highest peak:

Borah Peak 12,662 ft.

The Nez Perce are renowned breeders of the spotted horse known as the Appaloosa.

Idaho is a made-up name. It is believed that a politician named George M. Willing invented the word. In 1860, Willing told the United States Congress that Idaho was a Native American word meaning "gem of the mountains." He wanted to name the Colorado region Idaho, but the name was rejected when Congress learned that Idaho was not a Native American term after all. Meanwhile, the word had spread north, and mines at the Clearwater and Salmon Rivers became known as the Idaho Mines. As a result of the popularity of the name, Congress was forced to reconsider its earlier decision. In 1863, the vast region including all of present-day Idaho, Montana, and Wyoming, was named the Idaho Territory.

Within the next few years, the vast distances between the mining communities forced the separation of the Idaho Territory. By 1868, both Montana and Wyoming had become their own territories, and Idaho gained its present borders. Idaho is the only state name to be invented out of thin air.

QUICK FACTS

Idaho's state horse is the Appaloosa.

The syringa is Idaho's official state flower. It is a wildflower that grows in clusters of white blossoms.

The Idaho star garnet is the state gemstone. It is a rare gem, found only in Idaho and **Indochina.**

Among Idaho's most important rivers are the Snake, the Salmon, the Clearwater, and the Payette.

Nestled in the Idaho mountains, the Sun Valley ski resort has 2,054 acres of skiable terrain. It has been voted the number one ski resort in the United States.

The Thunder Mountain Railroad Line passes through the shortest solid rock railroad tunnel in the nation.

Other nicknames for Idaho include "The Potato State" and "The Spud State."

The mountain bluebird is Idaho's state bird. It can usually be found nesting in rock crevices or inside holes in trees.

The monarch butterfly became the state insect in 1992.

In 1864, both the Northern Pacific and the Union Pacific railroads laid track in the area. This made it easier for new settlers to travel to the region. The railroads also began to ship out Idaho's minerals, lumber, and farm products. Soon, large communities sprang up. By 1890, the year that it became a state, Idaho's population had risen to about 90,000 people. Thanks to mining, forestry, and farming, its economy was thriving.

Today, Idaho is well known for its potatoes. Vast potato fields spread across the southeastern part of the state. Idaho produces far more potatoes than any other state in the country. Idaho potatoes account for one-third of the national potato production and can be found on dinner tables all over the world. Idaho is also home to powerful **corporations** that make great advances in technology, while the state's forests and mines supply precious natural resources.

Potatoes contribute about $2.5 billion to the state's economy.

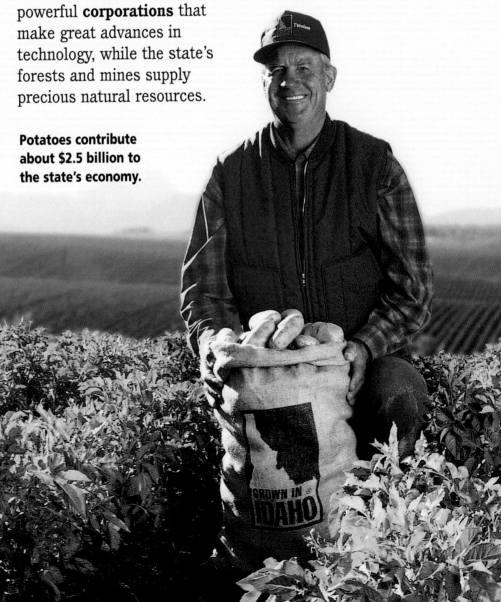

The Snake River stretches nearly 490 miles across southern Idaho. Idaho has more miles of rivers than any other state—3,100 miles.

LAND AND CLIMATE

Idaho's landscape is both beautiful and varied. Towering mountains, vast sand dunes, deep river canyons, underground ice caves, and prehistoric lava beds contribute to the state's diverse beauty.

In contrast to the densely forested mountains is the Snake River Plain. This plain sweeps across southern Idaho in an arc that covers the width of the state. It is a broad, treeless expanse of land that includes some of the most desolate areas of the northwestern United States.

Idaho's climate is mild. Winds from the Pacific Ocean bring warm sea air to the state, and the high mountains along the eastern border block out cold winter winds coming from the north and the east. Idaho summers are generally warm, with hotter temperatures occurring in the plains and valleys. The mountains are usually cooler and wetter throughout the year. In winter, the mountains can receive enormous amounts of snow.

Winchester Lake is a beautiful 103-acre lake at the foot of the Craig Mountains.

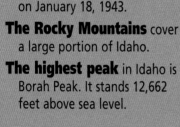

QUICK FACTS

North America's deepest gorge is in Idaho. Hells Canyon is situated on the Idaho–Oregon border, and reaches a depth of 1.5 miles.

The hottest temperature ever recorded in Idaho was at Orofino on July 28, 1934. It was 118° Fahrenheit. The coldest temperature ever recorded in the state was –60°F at Island Park Dam on January 18, 1943.

The Rocky Mountains cover a large portion of Idaho.

The highest peak in Idaho is Borah Peak. It stands 12,662 feet above sea level.

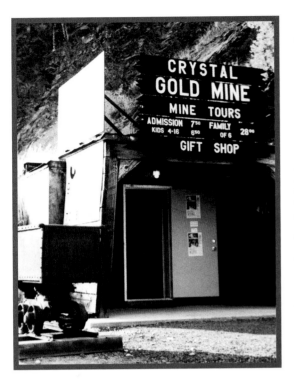

The Crystal Gold Mine is open to tourists. Gold was first discovered here by Tom Irwin in 1879.

NATURAL RESOURCES

Natural resources have long been the basis for Idaho's economy. Water is the most important of these resources. More than 2,000 lakes combine with five large river systems to supply the state with plenty of water for **hydroelectric** power, **irrigation**, and recreation.

Water plays an essential role in Idaho's agricultural production. The most fertile soil in the state is found in the Snake River Plain region. Since the region is very dry, an irrigation system has been constructed to bring water to the area. When irrigated, the soils in the Snake River Plain can produce crops of wheat, fruit, potatoes, and other vegetables. Soils in other parts of the state are not as well suited for farming. Some sections of the Snake River Plain are completely infertile, and soils in the mountain regions are thin and unable to sustain crops.

Idaho's mountains are home to another valuable resource—minerals. Valuable mineral deposits can be found in all of Idaho's counties. Silver, gold, lead, and phosphate are among the most important mineral resources in the state.

Many of Idaho's farms rely on irrigation systems. The state is second only to California in the amount of water used to irrigate crops.

Buttercups are common wildflowers in the moist regions of Idaho. They can be found around lakes and in forested mountain ranges.

QUICK FACTS

There are ten National Forests in Idaho.

Idaho's state tree is the western white pine. It is found in abundance north of the Clearwater River.

Idaho's tallest western white pine is located near Elk River. It stands about 219 feet tall.

The northernmost part of Idaho is called the Panhandle because its shape resembles the handle of a pan. This area is known for its many lakes, forests, and mineral resources.

At the Shoshone Ice Caves, air currents have formed amazing ice sculptures in a natural lava tube.

PLANTS AND ANIMALS

People in Idaho enjoy some of the largest unspoiled natural areas in the United States. Vast evergreen forests cover nearly 40 percent of the state. These forests are mostly on mountainous terrain and contain Douglas firs, pines, spruces, and western larches. Idaho's valleys contain birches, willows, and aspens. Some of the state's red cedar trees are hundreds of years old.

Much of southwestern Idaho is too dry for large trees to survive. Instead, sagebrush and bunchgrass fill the land. Fireweeds, goldenrods, and lilies are common flowering plants in the dry areas, while water-loving plants in the state include skunk cabbages and pond lilies. Mosses, ferns, and wildflowers grow all over the state. Several species of orchids grow deep in the forests, and violets and buttercups cover mountain meadows in spring and summer.

More than 21 million acres of forests cover Idaho.

Otters may feed on a variety of animals from small mammals to frogs and birds.

Idaho's natural areas are home to all kinds of animals. It is one of the few places in the United States where many large mammals still roam free. Moose, grizzly and black bears, elk, cougar, and caribou live in Idaho's forests. Some smaller animals living in the forests include beavers, minks, otters, muskrats, and raccoons. Mule deer and white-tailed deer can be found throughout the state, and many types of fish swim in Idaho's lakes and rivers.

Idaho is careful to preserve its nature and wildlife. The Snake River Birds of Prey Natural Conservation Area is home to the world's largest concentration of nesting raptors. Eagles, ospreys, hawks, and falcons make their homes in this protected area. Other wildlife preserves in the state include the Grays Lake National Wildlife Refuge and the Kootenai Wildlife Refuge. The Frank Church–River of No Return Wilderness Area is a huge protected region that covers about 2 million acres of forest in the northwestern part of the state.

QUICK FACTS

The cutthroat trout is the state fish of Idaho. It can be found swimming in many of the state's rivers and lakes. It earned its name from the colorful slash on the underside of its jaw.

The World Center for Birds of Prey, started in 1984, is located in Boise. The center breeds more than 200 falcons, condors, and eagles for release into the wild.

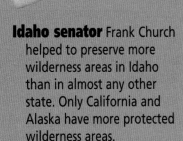

Idaho senator Frank Church helped to preserve more wilderness areas in Idaho than in almost any other state. Only California and Alaska have more protected wilderness areas.

The average bear in Idaho will eat 20 to 25 pounds of berries, grass, brush, insects, and meat per day.

The Sierra Silver Mine offers tours to those interested in Idaho's mining history.

The Old Idaho Penitentiary, in Boise, is open to visitors. The jail functioned for 103 years and housed some of the state's worst criminals. It closed its doors in 1973.

Balanced Rock is another natural **phenomenon** that attracts tourists. Through the ages, the bottom section of the massive rock has been worn away, giving the impression that it might fall over at any minute.

Silver City, southwest of Boise, is a real ghost town. Visitors can walk along the empty streets and inspect the old, rustic buildings where miners and their families once lived.

TOURISM

Visitors from all over the world come to Idaho to see its many natural wonders, breathe its fresh air, and explore its towering mountains. In Idaho, you can enjoy almost any kind of outdoor recreation.

Idaho's caves are popular attractions. At the Crystal Ice Cave, visitors can descend into the heart of a dead volcano and find fascinating ice formations. At Minnetonka Cave, visitors can walk through beautiful limestone rooms created by underground rivers. A different sort of cave can be explored at the old Sierra Silver Mine in Coeur d'Alene. There, tourists can explore an underground mine and experience what it was like to be a miner over a century ago.

One of Idaho's most popular natural wonders is Craters of the Moon National Monument. This area, in the eastern half of the Snake River Plain, is one of the most unusual geological formations in the United States. Volcanic eruptions and lava flows began at this site about 15,000 years ago, and continued until about 2,000 years ago. Today, visitors can explore the remains of these eruptions.

The Craters of the Moon was established as a National Monument in 1924.

Idaho accounts for more than 30 percent of the potatoes produced in the United States. The average citizen eats 142 pounds of potatoes per year.

INDUSTRY

Idaho's agricultural industry is an important part of the state's economy, employing about 13 percent of the state's workers. Idaho's potatoes are the state's leading crop. Wheat is the state's second most important crop. Idaho farmers also harvest barley, sugar beets, and beans.

Idaho's manufacturing industry also contributes to the state's economy. Food processing is one of the leading manufacturing activities. Idaho boasts over twenty potato-processing plants. People all over North America enjoy French fries that were processed in Idaho. Other food processing plants in the state include beet-sugar refineries, meat and poultry processors, dairies, and canning and freezing companies. Most of these plants are located in the southern part of the state, near the agricultural areas. The Boise area is active in the manufacturing of high technology products such as computers and computer software.

QUICK FACTS

In the 1940s, Idaho millionaire J. R. Simplot thought of ways to add value to the potato. Some of his ideas included freezing, drying, and frying the spuds.

The Silver Valley, in northern Idaho, is one of the top ten mining districts in the world. More than $4 billion of precious metals have been mined since 1884.

Boise is currently the corporate headquarters for industry giants such as Albertsons, Hewlett-Packard, and Micron Technology.

One of the largest sawmills in the world is located in the city of Lewiston.

More than 60 percent of Idaho's potatoes are processed into frozen or dried potato products, which are then exported.

Boise Cascade is headquartered in Boise. The company owns or controls more than 2 million acres of timberland.

GOODS AND SERVICES

Idaho produces a vast number of wood products such as plywood, poles, boxes, furniture, and railroad ties. Wood pulp and paper are also produced in the state. The majority of the state's lumber mills are located in the Panhandle.

Most of Idaho's main exports, such as farm products, minerals, and lumber travel out of the state by train. Other products are shipped by **barge**. Lewiston, in the north, is the major port town. In fact, it is known as "The Seaport of Idaho" even though it is almost 500 miles from the Pacific Ocean. In 1915, engineers built a canal on the Columbia River, and a series of dams and **locks** on both the Columbia and Snake Rivers. These allowed barges and tugboats to transport farm and forest products out of Lewiston to the Pacific Ocean. Today, large ships still carry grain and lumber out of Lewiston.

Canals along the Columbia River allow ships to transport goods between Idaho and the Pacific Ocean.

More than 15,000 students attend the Boise State University.

Idahoans can read up on current events in one of ten daily newspapers published in the state. Idaho's oldest newspaper is the *Idaho Statesman*. It was founded in 1864 and is still in circulation. Other daily newspapers include the Twin-Falls *Times-News*, the *Coeur d'Alene Press*, and the *Lewiston Morning Tribune*.

Idaho is home to a number of private and public colleges, and three major universities—Boise State University, Idaho State University, and the University of Idaho. Many of the educational programs in Idaho are related to the state's livelihood. At the University of Idaho students can earn degrees in mining and forestry. The College for Agriculture, which is part of the University of Idaho, has improved the state's farming output. Over the years, students and researchers in the agricultural programs have developed new and improved varieties of wheat, barley, oats, and other important crops.

New farming practices, developed by the University of Idaho, have helped make agriculture a thriving state industry. About 13.5 million acres of farmland cover the state.

Ancient petroglyphs and pictographs can be seen at Hells Canyon National Recreation Area.

FIRST NATIONS

Idaho's earliest inhabitants lived thousands of years ago. While digging in southern Idaho's Wilson Butte Cave, **archeologists** discovered pieces of pottery, jagged arrowheads, and other tools. These items were well over 13,000 years old. Other areas of the state also contain proof of early cultures. Ancient rock carvings called **petroglyphs** and rock drawings called **pictographs** can be found along the Salmon and Snake Rivers and in other regions of the state.

By the early nineteenth century, seven main groups of Native Peoples inhabited the Idaho region. The Coeur d'Alene, Pend d'Oreille, and Kootenai lived in the north. The Nez Perce lived in the central region of the state, and the Shoshone, Bannock, and Paiute lived in the south. These groups relied on Idaho's natural resources. They hunted wildlife in the forests and prairies, and fished in the region's many lakes and rivers.

The name Nez Perce means "pierced nose" in French. French explorers mistakenly gave this name to the Nez Perce after encountering another tribe. In fact, the Nez Perce never pierced their noses or wore ornaments.

QUICK FACTS

Native Peoples in Idaho saw their first horse in the 1700s. It forever changed their lives. Horses gave the Native Peoples greater mobility while hunting and made it easier to trade with Native groups from other northwestern states.

The largest of Idaho's Native-American groups were the Nez Perce and the Shoshone.

Cradleboards, made of buckskins and willows, were used by the Shoshone to keep their babies warm and secure while traveling.

Reverend Henry Spalding was the first person to grow potatoes in Idaho.

Idaho was the last of the fifty states to be explored by people of European descent.

Sacagawea, a young Shoshone woman, was born in Idaho. She traveled with Lewis and Clark and acted as an interpreter between the explorers and the Native Peoples.

Lewis and Clark reported that the Idaho region had many fur-bearing animals. Soon after Lewis and Clark left, fur traders began to explore the area. Fur-trading companies established trading routes and posts.

Meriwether Lewis

EXPLORERS AND MISSIONARIES

Explorers Meriwether Lewis and William Clark were the first people of European descent to explore the Idaho region. In 1805, President Thomas Jefferson sent Lewis and Clark on an **expedition** to search for a water route to the Pacific Ocean. The explorers sailed up the Missouri River. They traveled through Idaho's challenging Bitterroot Mountains. The journey was difficult and they endured many hardships along the way, including drastic food shortages and deep snow.

During the 1830s, missionaries from the eastern United States became interested in the Idaho region. In 1836, Henry and Eliza Spalding arrived in the area. The Spaldings established the first mission in Idaho, near present-day Lewiston. They exchanged farming techniques with the Nez Perce and built Idaho's first **gristmill**, blacksmith shop, and printing shop.

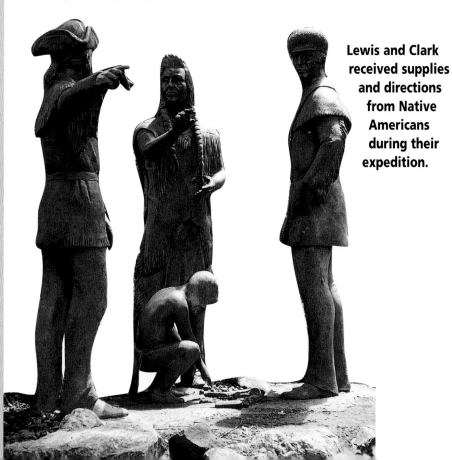

Lewis and Clark received supplies and directions from Native Americans during their expedition.

In Idaho, the Oregon Trail followed the Snake River to Salmon Falls, and then north, past Fort Boise towards Oregon.

EARLY SETTLERS

During the 1840s and 1850s, an estimated 53,000 **immigrants** passed through the Idaho region, but very few of them actually settled in the area. They were moving westward along the Oregon Trail to the fertile farmland of Oregon and the rich gold fields of California.

On April 14, 1860, over twenty Mormon families came to Idaho from Utah and founded what was to become Idaho's first permanent settlement. The town of Franklin was situated in the southeastern part of the state, and the settlers worked hard to survive in their new home. They dug irrigation ditches, and proved that the dry soil in the southern region could be used for farming. Other Mormon pioneers soon settled in southern parts of the state.

QUICK FACTS

In 1846, Great Britain gave up its claim to the lands south of the Canada–United States border. The Idaho region was now officially under United States ownership and was considered part of the vast Oregon Territory.

At first, Native Peoples were receptive to the new settlers. As time went on, many problems arose. **Treaties** forced Native Peoples onto reservations, and new settlements reduced their farming and grazing land. This led to fights between the Native Peoples and the United States Army. Many people lost their lives during these battles.

Idaho was a popular destination for Mormon settlers. Today, more than half of Idaho's church-going population is Mormon.

During the 1860s, Idaho City was a gold-mining boom town with close to 40,000 residents. At the time, it was the largest town in the Pacific Northwest.

In 1900, a number of Wisconsin and Minnesota lumberjacks came to Idaho in the hopes of establishing a successful lumber industry.

Many Chinese people came to Idaho to work as miners during the gold rush.

Idaho City was one of the region's biggest mining settlements. It had saloons, theaters, and even an opera house.

In the same year that Franklin was founded, an important discovery was made in northern Idaho. Elias Pierce and his group of **prospectors** found a startling amount of gold at Orofino Creek in the Clearwater River region. News of this discovery had gold seekers from California and Oregon rushing to the region that they had previously ignored. Gold was found elsewhere in Idaho, and soon mining settlements sprung up throughout the territory. Ranchers, tradesmen, and merchants from other states saw the business potential in Idaho. They quickly followed the miners, setting up businesses in the various settlements.

Idaho's gold mining days were often quite rowdy. Violence and thefts were commonplace in many of the towns. On March 4, 1863, President Abraham Lincoln made Idaho a territory so that the government could bring order to its mining towns. Idaho's gold rush only lasted about ten years, but it provided the basis for permanent settlement in the region. People from other parts of the United States learned that Idaho had fertile farmlands, forests, and mineral resources.

In 1860, the discovery of silver and gold in Idaho resulted in a rush of prospectors and settlers from across the nation.

POPULATION

The Shoshone–Bannock Indian Festival is held during the second week of August. It is hosted by the Fort Hall Reservation.

Idaho is home to over 1.2 million people. Most Idahoans live in the farming areas of the south, or in the western half of the Panhandle. Mountainous areas in central and northern Idaho are nearly uninhabited. There are only a few remote communities in this wilderness. Transportation is difficult here, and supplies must be flown in by helicopters or small planes. Idaho's landscape has created a sense of **regionalism** within the state. Mountain ranges and desert areas are natural barriers that divide the state and isolate regions from one another.

Increasing opportunities in agriculture and industry are attracting newcomers from around the world. In fact, in the last decade, the state's population has increased by more than 28 percent. Idaho has a **population density** of 15.6 people per square mile. This is lower than the national population density of 77 people per square mile.

QUICK FACTS

Almost half of Idaho's population lives in one of the state's ten urban areas.

Most Idahoans live in the Snake River Valley region. It is the most populated region in the state.

Boise is Idaho's largest city, followed by Pocatello and Idaho Falls.

Boise

Idaho Cultural Groups

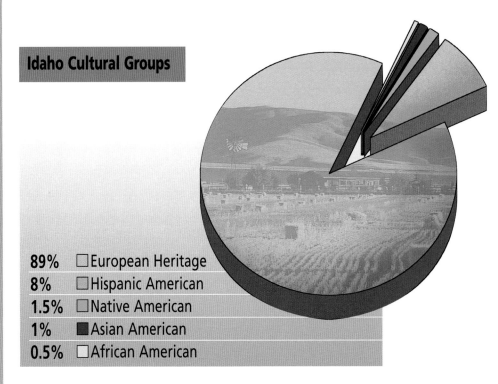

89% □ European Heritage
8% □ Hispanic American
1.5% □ Native American
1% ■ Asian American
0.5% □ African American

Lewiston, a thriving valley city of about 30,270 people, was named after the explorer Meriwether Lewis.

QUICK FACTS

Idaho has forty-four counties. A board of three elected commissioners governs each county.

In 1896, Idaho became the fourth state in the nation to give women the right to vote.

Idaho's government has three branches. The legislative branch creates new laws and examines Idaho's present laws. The judicial branch interprets these laws, and the executive branch puts the laws into action.

POLITICS AND GOVERNMENT

Idaho's mountain barriers have played a role in the political formation of the state. On March 4, 1863, Idaho was made a territory of the United States, with Lewiston as the capital. The vast distances and high mountains between communities made the government reconsider its decision to locate the capital in the north. In 1864, the capital was moved from Lewiston to Boise, which was larger and more accessible. People in northern Idaho were angry. Many of them felt that their political concerns would be ignored by the distant south.

Bigger problems were on the horizon. Because of its regional differences, some people thought the Idaho territory should not exist at all. In the mid-1880s, a plan to make northern Idaho part of Washington, and southern Idaho part of Nevada, was almost put into effect. Only a plea from the Idaho territorial governor, Edward A. Stevenson, prevented the plan from going forward. A few years later on July 3, 1890, Idaho became the forty-third state of the Union. Today, the state capital remains Boise, and Idaho's government works to keep the state united.

The State Capitol in Boise was closely modeled after the United States' Capitol.

CULTURAL GROUPS

Idaho pays tribute to its Basque heritage with the popular Sheepherders' Ball.

Idaho is proud of its rich heritage. All around the state there are exhibitions and festivals that celebrate its varied cultures. At the Idaho State Historical Museum, visitors can trace Idaho's history from the days of fur trading and mining camps to the development of Boise. The museum also puts special emphasis on Idaho's ethnic diversity, including Basque immigrants, Chinese miners, and Shoshone Native Americans.

The Basques are one of the most distinct ethnic groups in the state. During the 1800s, people from the Basque region of northern Spain came to Idaho. Many were experienced shepherds and were hired by sheep ranchers in the region. Today, most people of Basque descent live in the Boise area. They celebrate their traditions at festivals and on religious holidays. During the Sheepherders' Ball, Basques wear colorful costumes and play lively folk music.

QUICK FACTS

Idaho Spud Day is held every year in Shelly. The event celebrates Idaho's most important crop with a parade, music, and other special activities.

The Basque Museum and Cultural Center contains fascinating displays that describe the history, traditions, and unique language of the Basques.

Idaho's old mining days are recognized throughout the state with various festivals and museums. The Ketchum Wagon Days are an annual celebration of Idaho's mining heritage.

For the Sheepherders' Ball, hundreds of sheep are herded down Ketchum's main street and through the valley along Highway 75.

The Shoshone–Bannock Indian Festival features more than fifty arts, crafts, and food stands.

Many Native Americans in Idaho display great pride in their heritage. At the Fort Hall Reservation, near Pocatello, the Shoshone–Bannock Indian Festival celebrates traditional Native-American dress, dances, parades, crafts, and a rodeo. Lapwai's Nez Perce hold traditional dancing celebrations during Chief Looking Glass Days in August. The Coeur d'Alene Indian Pilgrimage also takes place in August. The annual pilgrimage brings the Coeur d'Alene back to the Cataldo Mission, which was built by their ancestors more than 140 years ago. After a mass, a dinner is held, followed by traditional dancing, singing, and drumming.

The gold rush of the 1860s brought many Chinese people to the Idaho region. When the gold rush ended, some stayed in the area to run businesses or to farm. Today, descendants of these early Chinese settlers continue to make their homes in Idaho. Chinese cultural events and festivities, such as Chinese New Year, take place in certain areas of the state.

The Cataldo Mission is the oldest-standing building in Idaho. It was built by missionaries and more than 300 Native Americans.

QUICK FACTS

A Hispanic Fiesta is held annually at Twin Falls. The fiesta celebrates Idaho's Hispanic heritage.

The Nez Perce National Historical Park Museum has an excellent collection of Nez Perce artifacts. A museum and a park preserve the history and culture of the Nez Perce.

The Nez Perce National Historical Park is really twenty-four sites spread across three states.

The Idaho Black History Museum, in Boise, opened in 1995.

QUICK FACTS

Boise is home to the Idaho Black History Museum. The museum was created to teach people about the history and culture of African Americans.

Every year the city of Rexburg holds the Idaho International Folk Dance Festival. It features talented folk dancers from around the world.

Boise's Morrison Center for the Performing Arts has an excellent arts program. The Boise Opera Company, Ballet Idaho, and the Boise Philharmonic all perform there.

During the summer, an outdoor **amphitheater** in Boise hosts the Idaho Shakespeare Festival.

ARTS AND ENTERTAINMENT

Idaho's early mining settlements had small theaters and opera houses where musical shows and plays were performed. Today, Idaho continues to celebrate and enjoy music, theater, and art.

Musical concerts and festivals take place throughout the year in Idaho. The Boise Philharmonic is the state's most prominent orchestra, but orchestras in Idaho Falls, Pocatello, and Moscow also entertain audiences with wonderful performances. Many of Idaho's colleges and universities also have impressive orchestras. In fact, many of the state's schools have strong music departments where students can develop their musical talents. The Lionel Hampton School of Music at the University of Idaho is a well-respected learning center. Each year, it hosts the famous Lionel Hampton Jazz Festival. Students from around the world come to perform for judges, listen to world-class jazz musicians, and learn from top jazz masters.

The University of Idaho's Lionel Hampton Jazz Festival attracts about 17,000 students from all over the United States and Canada.

The Northern Pacific Depot Railroad Museum was built at the turn of the century using mine tailings.

QUICK FACTS

The town of Wallace is home to the Northern Pacific Depot Railroad Museum, which celebrates the state's railroad heritage. The depot was used as a set for the 1979 movie *Heaven's Gate*.

Sculptor Gutzon Burglom was born in Idaho, near St. Charles. He is known for carving the faces of George Washington, Thomas Jefferson, Abraham Lincoln, and Theodore Roosevelt into Mount Rushmore, in South Dakota.

Ernest Hemingway worked on his classic novel *For Whom the Bell Tolls* while visiting Idaho. He fell in love with the state and spent his last years in Ketchum.

There is more to Idaho's music scene than the classical sounds of its orchestras or the cool beats of its jazz festivals. At the National Old Time Fiddlers Contest and Festival, audiences are treated to the lively tunes of some of the world's finest fiddlers. The event, which is held annually in Weiser, is considered one of the most important fiddling contests in the country. Idaho's strong folk-music tradition is on display at the state's many folk-music festivals.

Idaho delights in visual arts, too. The Boise Art Museum houses fine exhibits of national and international artwork. It features works by talented Idaho artists such as Thomas Martin, George W. Russell, and Margaret Brown. In addition to its permanent exhibits, the museum hosts an event called Art in the Park. This outdoor exhibition takes place each September in Boise's Julia Davis Park. It features the work of hundreds of artists from Idaho and around the world. The money raised from Art in the Park is used to maintain the museum and support Idaho artists.

Idaho's most talented artists are featured alongside international artists at the Boise Art Museum.

Kayaking is a popular way to enjoy the scenic surroundings of Redfish Lake. The lake is nestled in the middle of the Sawtooth Mountains.

SPORTS

Idaho is a great place for outdoor enthusiasts, nature lovers, and thrill seekers. Its towering mountains, shimmering lakes, and rapid rivers make it the ultimate outdoor playground. Throughout the spring and summer months, hikers and backpackers can trek along Idaho's mountain trails and camp in one of the state's many campgrounds. Swimmers can go for a dip in one of the many beautiful lakes in northern Idaho, or further south in the lakes of the Sawtooth National Recreation Area. Idaho's lakes are also perfect for sailing, fishing, or canoeing.

More adventurous water lovers can raft, canoe, or kayak on one of the state's quick-flowing rivers. Licensed outfitters offer guided river-rafting trips down many of the state's rushing waterways. Experienced kayakers come to the state to ride the white-water rapids of the Selway, Salmon, or Snake rivers.

QUICK FACTS

Idaho has no major league sports teams.

Talented football star Jerry Kramer attended the University of Idaho. He played for the Green Bay Packers from 1958 to 1968 as an offensive lineman and kicker.

Picabo Street, from Triumph, is a world-champion downhill skier. She won a gold medal at the 1998 Winter Olympics in Nagano and a silver medal at the 1994 Olympics in Lillehammer.

The Sun Valley resort boasts four golf courses and eighty-five tennis courts.

The Sun Valley resort is a popular destination in both summer and winter. Summertime activities include horseback riding, swimming, biking, and hiking.

Schweitzer Mountain's high-speed six-passenger chairlift takes less than 6 minutes and carries 2,000 skiers to the summit per hour.

During the winter months, Idaho has some of the best skiing in North America. Among the state's most popular ski resorts are Silver Mountain, Schweitzer Mountain, and Bogus Basin. There are many ski resorts in the state, catering to beginners and advanced skiers alike. Olympians such as Christin Cooper and Bill Johnson have trained on Idaho's slopes.

Sun Valley, which opened in 1936, is the state's most famous ski resort. It offers its visitors excellent downhill and cross-country ski trails. It also has trails for snowshoeing and snowmobiling, and plenty of spots for ice skating. In fact, the resort boasts a world-class ice skating rink where Olympic medalists such as Kristi Yamaguchi, Brian Boitano, and Nancy Kerrigan have performed to sold-out crowds.

The Idaho Winter Games, held in Boise, caters to those outdoor enthusiasts with a competitive edge. This winter sports festival gathers more than 2,500 state and regional amateur athletes in such events as freestyle skiing, snowboarding, ice hockey, figure skating, snowmobiling, and alpine and cross-country ski races.

QUICK FACTS

A Ketchum resident named Dick Fosbury invented the popular high jump technique known as the Fosbury Flop.

Harmon Killebrew is a talented baseball player from Payette. He signed with the Washington Senators when he was only 17 years old. Killebrew ranks fifth on the all-time list of home-run hitters. In 1984, Killebrew was inducted into the Baseball Hall of Fame.

Snowmobiling is another way to enjoy the beauty of Sun Valley.

Brain Teasers

1

True or False: There are over thirty different license plate designs for the state of Idaho.

Answer: True. The most popular design features a crimson sunset with forests and mountains.

2

True or False: Early moon-mission astronauts used to train at Craters of the Moon.

Answer: True. Astronauts trained at Craters of the Moon because of its moon-like terrain.

3

Which of the following is not a town in Idaho?

a. Moscow

b. Atlanta

c. Paris

d. Milan

Answer: d. Milan

4

True or False: On October 28, 1983, Borah Peak grew 1 foot higher.

Answer: True. On that day, a huge earthquake shook the mountain and lifted it 1 foot higher.

5

Which of the following was invented in Rigby?

a. The microwave

b. The television

c. The cellular phone

d. The wheel

Answer: b. Rigby is the hometown of Philo T. Farnsworth, the pioneer of television technology.

6

True or False: The world's first alpine skiing chairlift is located in Sun Valley.

Answer: True. The chairlift was adapted from a device that was used to load bananas onto boats.

7

What Idaho city was named for its many trees?

Answer: Boise. In the early nineteenth century, French fur trappers were in awe of the number of trees in the area, and are believed to have named it after "les bois," which means "the woods." Today, Boise is known as the City of Trees.

8

Can an Idaho citizen give a fellow Idahoan a 51-pound box of candy?

Answer: No. Oddly enough, it is illegal in Idaho to give a box of candy that weighs more than 50 pounds.

FOR MORE INFORMATION

Books

Fradin, Dennis Brindell. *Idaho*. Sea to Shining Sea series. Chicago: Children's Press: 1995.

Kent, Zachary. *Idaho*. America the Beautiful series. Chicago: Children's Press: 1990.

Pelta, Kathy. *Idaho.* Hello U.S.A. series. Minneapolis: Lerner, 1995.

Web sites

You can also go online and have a look at the following Web sites:

State of Idaho
http://www.state.id.us

Idaho Department of Commerce
http://www.idoc.state.id.us

Craters of the Moon National Monument
http://www.nps.gov/crmo

Sun Valley Resort
http://www.sunvalley.com

Some Web sites stay current longer than others. To find other Idaho Web sites, enter search terms, such as "Idaho," "Boise," "Gem State," or any other topic you want to research.

GLOSSARY

archeologists: scientists who study ancient cultures by examining their ruins and remains

amphitheater: a semi-circular seating arrangement, around a stage

barge: a flat-bottomed boat that carries large shipments of goods on canals or rivers

corporations: large companies

expedition: a journey made for exploration

gorge: a steep and narrow valley

gristmill: a mill that grinds grain

hydroelectric: energy created by moving water

immigrants: people who have come to settle in one country from another

Indochina: a region of southeast Asia that consists of Myanmar (Burma), Thailand, Laos, Cambodia, and Vietnam

irrigation: supply of water to dry regions through channels

locks: chambers, in a canal or dam, which lower or raise the water level so that ships may pass through

petroglyphs: ancient carvings on rock

phenomenon: a naturally occurring event

pictographs: ancient paintings or drawings on rock

population density: the average number of people per unit of area

precious: of great value

prospectors: people who search for valuable mineral deposits

regionalism: pride in one's own region

transcontinental: crossing or stretching across a continent

treaties: formal agreements between two or more governments

INDEX